EDGE
BOOKS

T0040600

MONSTER HANDBOOKS

VAMPIRES

◆ The Truth Behind ◆
HISTORY'S CREEPIEST BLOODSUCKERS

by Alicia Z. Klepeis

Consultant:
David Gilmore, Professor of Anthropology
Stony Brook University, New York

CAPSTONE PRESS
a capstone imprint

Edge Books are published by Capstone Press,
1710 Roe Crest Drive, North Mankato, Minnesota 56003.
www.capstonepub.com

Library of Congress Cataloging-in-Publication Data
Klepeis, Alicia, 1971– author.
Vampires : the truth behind history's creepiest bloodsuckers / by Alicia Z. Klepeis.
pages cm.—(Edge books. Monster handbooks)
Summary: "Describes ancient history, medieval lore, and modern portrayals of vampires in
today's popular culture"—Provided by publisher.
Audience: 8–12.
Audience: Grades 4–6.
Includes bibliographical references and index.
ISBN 978-1-4914-4250-0 (library binding)
ISBN 978-1-4914-4335-4 (paperback)
ISBN 978-1-4914-4311-8 (ebook PDF)
1. Vampires—Juvenile literature. 2. Vampires—History—Juvenile literature. 3. Vampires in
literature—Juvenile literature. I. Title.
BF1556.K54 2016
398'.45—dc23   2015001429

Editorial Credits
Aaron Sautter, editor; Bobbie Nuytten, designer; Gina Kammer, media researcher;
Laura Manthe, production specialist

Photo Credits
Alamy: © Jack Carey, 21; Bridgeman Images: Pictures From History/Philippines: An aswang or
vampire-like mythical creature of the Philippines as represented by Juan de Plazcensia in the late
15th century, 8, Private Collection/Dracula Claims Lucy, 2009 (oil on canvas), Barry, Jonathan
(Contemporary Artist), 5; Corbis: 10, © Bettmann, 17, 25, © John Springer Collection, 28, ©
Leemage, 18; Getty Images: Hulton Archive, 23; Granger, NYC: ullstein bild, 15; Newscom:
Album/20TH CENTURY FOX TV, 26, KRT/RON COHEN, 29, ZUMA Press/Ropi/Boma,
12; Science Source: 13; Shutterstock: Alexey Painter, cover, Alexey Painter, 4, Fabiana Ponzi,
27, Ginger Ale, (bats) 29, Golubentsev, 7, hagit berkovich, 6, JMicic, (hands) 9, Lasha Kilasonia,
(Earth map) 9, MaraZe, 16, Michael Wick, 19, Radek Sturgolewski, 24, Sarun T, 14, Taeya18, 30,
Zacarias Pereira da Mata, cover, 1

Design Elements
Shutterstock: blue pencil (calligraphic designs), Ensuper (grunge background), Gordan (grunge
frames), Slava Gerj (grunge scratched background)

Printed in China by Nordica
0415/CA21500562
032015   008844NORDF15

Table of Contents

Creepy, Undead Bloodsuckers

Night is approaching. Darkness closes in over a crumbling old castle. Slowly, a coffin opens. A shadowy mist emerges and floats toward an open window. In an instant, the mist transforms into a huge black bat that flies off toward the nearby village. What is this monstrous creature? It's a vampire—and it's looking for a fresh meal of blood!

Vampires have long been terrifying, **undead** creatures of the night. Vampires in today's books and movies are often handsome men or beautiful women. However, vampire stories through history usually described them as creepy, yet cunning, monsters. They were technically dead, but still prowled around at night hunting for fresh blood. Vampires in several tales even had the power to **hypnotize** their victims, making them easy prey. Take a walk through history and see how stories about these creepy monsters have changed over time.

undead—no longer alive but still able to move and take action

hypnotize—to put a person into a sleeplike state

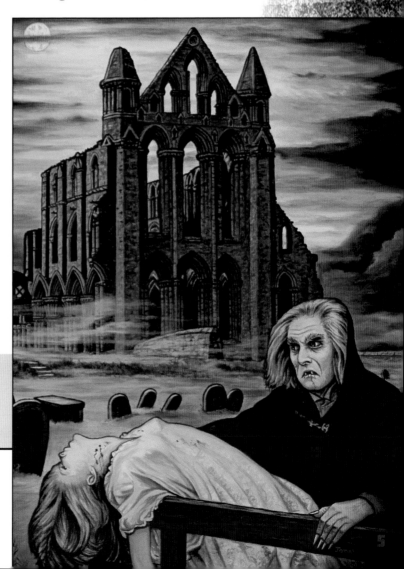

Bloodsucking vampires enjoy hypnotizing and feeding on the blood of beautiful young women in many tales.

CHAPTER 1
Vampires in the Ancient World

Bloodsucking vampires have lived in people's imaginations for thousands of years. People in the ancient world often blamed vampires for diseases, unnatural deaths, and other events they didn't understand. In ancient stories about vampires, these undead monsters spread fear and chaos wherever they went.

THE FIRST VAMPIRES

Many people believe the first vampire myths began in ancient Babylon. The Babylonians believed in a female demon called *Lilitu*. This creature was said to be the bearer of disease, illness, and death. It usually looked like a normal human woman. But it had a nasty habit of feasting on the blood of babies.

FACT: The *otgiruru* from Namibian legends was a vampirelike dog. Sometimes it howled and pretended to be a family pet that was injured. When someone came to its aid, the creature viciously attacked the person.

The ancient Assyrians had bloodthirsty monsters called *ekimmu*. These creatures were thought to be the restless spirits of people who died violently or who weren't buried properly. Some *ekimmu* were described as thin, sickly people. But others supposedly appeared as winged demons or simply as rushing wind. *Ekimmu* were known to drink the blood of people who were near death.

Stories from ancient Greece and Rome featured terrifying monsters called *strix*. Blocking a *strix* from a person's home was said to be impossible. Legends stated that no barriers or locks could keep them out. These terrible creatures usually flew around at night, looking to drink the blood of children.

Strix *were said to be female shape-shifters that could turn into birds of prey such as owls.*

ANCIENT ASIAN VAMPIRES

Ancient Asian **folklore** featured several types of creepy bloodsucking monsters. *Aswangs* were shape-shifting vampires in the Philippines. By day they usually looked like beautiful young women. But at night they often turned into animals, such as large birds, bats, or dogs. These creatures enjoyed eating the bloody hearts and livers of their victims.

The *churel* from India was a gruesome creature. Its feet were turned backward, with the toes in back and the heel in front. Many stories described a *churel* as a woman who died during childbirth. This creature sometimes appeared as a beautiful woman to trap its victims. Young men were especially defenseless against a *churel's* charms.

folklore—tales, sayings, and customs among a group of people

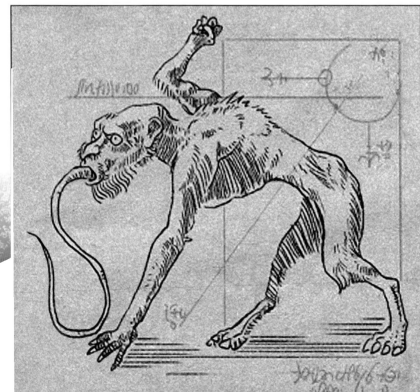

Aswangs *used long, pointed tongues to pierce people's necks and drink their blood.*

ROME
strix
shape-shifter that turned into a bird of prey; supposedly no barriers or locks on doors could keep them out

GREECE/ROME
lamia
half woman and half snake; sucked the blood of men

BABYLON
Lilitu
a demon that appeared as a human woman; drank the blood of babies

ASSYRIA
ekimmu
appeared as sickly people, winged demons, or rushing wind; drank the blood of people near death

CHINA
jiang-shi
strong and vicious, had super-long eyebrows used to magically trap victims

PHILIPPINES
aswang
could turn into a bird and hide in trees; long, pointed tongue could prick a victim's neck from a long distance away

GREECE
keres (Ceres)
preyed on ill people; grabbed victims with large claws or talons; were said to escape from jars used to hold the bodies of the dead

INDIA
churel
feet were backward with heel in front and toes in back; their beauty easily attracted male victims

MALAYSIA
langsuir
female vampire that sucked blood through a hole in the back of its neck; preferred to drink babies' blood

AUSTRALIA
yara-ma-yha-who
hid in fig trees to attack people who camped under them

CHAPTER 2
Medieval Vampire Folklore

In the Middle Ages (about AD 500 to 1450), most people were uneducated and understood little about death. During this period the **plague** killed millions of people across Europe. With imaginations running wild, people often believed that vampires were responsible for so much death and suffering.

Also known as the Black Death, tens of millions of people across Europe died from the plague in the mid-1300s.

FACT: Sometimes people with a disease called rabies were thought to be vampires. Infected people often had red foam on their lips. Medieval people thought this was because the infected people had just dined on blood. But we now know the red foam came from excess saliva, not a bloody feast!

MISTAKEN FOR VAMPIRES

A dead body's appearance may have led some **medieval** people to believe in vampires. A dead body can become bloated from a buildup of gases inside of it. The gases can also force blood to trickle out of the body's eyes, nose, or mouth. It's easy to see how medieval people could make mistakes about such bloody, bloated bodies. They often thought the bodies were undead vampires who had just fed on living people's blood.

Dead bodies had other signs that led people to mistake them for vampires. When a body **decomposes**, its skin shrinks back as it dries out. This process causes the hair and teeth to appear to grow longer. These "signs of life" helped convince believers that the bodies were vampires that had cheated death.

plague—a disease that spreads quickly and kills most people who catch it

medieval—having to do with the period of European history between AD 500 and 1450

decompose—to rot or decay

BECOMING A VAMPIRE

There were many ways people could become vampires in medieval stories. In some places it was thought that people could be born as vampires. In Russia if a baby was born with a split lower lip, it was considered to be a vampire. In Romania hair on the front or back of a newborn baby was also a sign of vampirism. And in some parts of central Europe, a baby born with visible teeth was believed to be a vampire.

Medieval folklore described several other ways that people could become vampires. One legend said that if a black cat crossed an expectant mother's path, her baby would be born a vampire. People with red hair and blue eyes in Romania were often suspected to be vampires. In some places it was thought that people could become vampires if they died before being **baptized** as Christians. This could also happen if dead people didn't receive a proper Christian burial.

baptize—to pour water on someone as part of a Christian religious practice

FACT: Medieval people sometimes stuffed objects into the mouths of dead bodies to prevent them from becoming vampires. Some of these objects included garlic, dirt, gold coins, crosses, and even bricks.

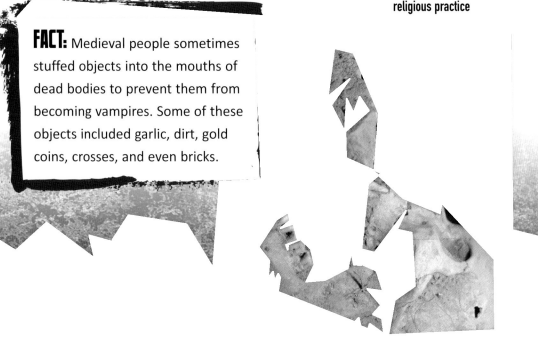

Author Bram Stoker wrote his famous novel *Dracula* in the late 1800s. Stoker based much of his story on European folktales about vampires. But he was also influenced by a terrifying figure from history.

Vlad Tepes, also known as "Vlad the Impaler," was born in Transylvania around 1431. When he grew up, Vlad took the last name of Dracula, which means "son of the dragon." Eventually Vlad became the ruler over the region of Walachia in Romania.

Vlad was a brutal leader. He used many horrible punishments against his enemies. His favorite method was to **impale** people on wooden stakes and leave them to die. Vlad soon earned the name of Tepes, or "The Impaler." During his six-year rule, it's thought that he ordered at least 40,000 people to be killed by impaling.

There are no known records of Vlad drinking blood. However, some documents state that he enjoyed eating his meals among the bloody, impaled bodies of his victims.

impale—to thrust a sharpened stake through a person's body

BLOODTHIRSTY HUNTERS

In many medieval tales, vampires slept in their graves from sunrise to sunset. Bright sunlight supposedly weakened them and their powers. This weakness forced vampires to hunt for blood at night and return to their graves before dawn. However, prowling for victims in the dark also helped them hide their evil deeds.

Several stories stated that vampires were shape-shifters that could take different forms. They could turn into animals such as bats or wolves. Sometimes they could even turn into a misty form and slip under locked doors to reach sleeping victims. Other legends said that vampires couldn't enter a home without first being invited in.

FACT: Greek tales describe vampires called *vrykolakas*. These creatures didn't seek blood like most vampires. They instead spread disease by knocking on people's doors. If someone opened the door after the first knock, the monster would disappear. But the victim would be infected and die within a few days to become a new vrykolakas. For this reason, many people in Greece today refuse to answer the door unless someone knocks twice.

Biting a victim's neck was a common method of vampire attack in many stories. After being bitten, the victim usually went into a **trance**. Without treatment, the victim would waste away and die. Then after a short time, they'd rise from the dead to seek out fresh blood as a newly born vampire.

trance—a conscious state in which someone is not really aware of what is happening

In the story of Nosferatu, the vampire's victims are unable to resist his supernatural powers.

CHAPTER 3
Medieval Monster Hunting

Medieval vampires were thought to be ruthless and cunning hunters. However, there were ways that people could protect themselves. Stories were full of defenses people could use against the bloodthirsty monsters. The Middle Ages also saw the rise of professional vampire hunters. These highly skilled people were hired to track down and destroy suspected vampires.

VAMPIRE WEAKNESSES

Vampires in European folklore had several weaknesses. For example, they supposedly hated garlic. To keep vampires away, people often hung strings of garlic around their homes. They also rubbed raw garlic around the windows, doors, and chimneys of their homes.

Many medieval people thought that garlic had magical powers against supernatural monsters such as vampires.

People also believed that vampires were evil and unholy creatures. They used holy water or religious symbols, such as Christian **crucifixes**, to drive vampires away.

Vampires were also said to be obsessed with counting things. Several European tales described how people used this weakness to their advantage. They scattered tiny seeds along the road between the graveyard and their homes. They believed that vampires would spend all their time collecting and counting the seeds, rather than hunting for new victims. People often sprinkled seeds or sand around their beds for this same reason.

A holy crucifix was thought to have the power to defeat a vampire's evil nature.

crucifix—a symbol of the beliefs of Christians

HUNTING VAMPIRES

Many people in the Middle Ages believed that professional vampire hunters could help deal with suspected vampires. These hunters often lurked in cemeteries at night to look for signs of vampire activity. If they saw an eerie, bluish light, it was considered to be a sign of a **soul** wandering out of its grave. A fresh grave with a hole dug through it was even stronger evidence of vampire activity. And a crooked gravestone or cross could also indicate the presence of a vampire.

soul—the spiritual part of a person

Vampire hunters were thought to have the skills needed to track down and destroy evil vampires.

Hunters had a few other methods to find vampires. They might scatter salt around the grave of a suspected vampire. If the creature left its grave, it would leave footprints in the salt. Hunters also used animals to detect the undead creatures. Horses were thought to be sensitive to supernatural spirits. If a horse refused to step over a grave, it meant that a vampire could be inside it.

In some stories vampire hunters used dogs or white wolves to track down suspected vampires.

DESTROYING EVIL VAMPIRES

Hunters in vampire stories had several ways to defend themselves from the evil bloodsuckers. A few hunters carried guns loaded with silver bullets, which were thought to be deadly to a vampire. Hunters also carried containers of holy water, which was believed to burn vampires' flesh.

Medieval people believed that a vampire could be destroyed in several ways. One method involved cutting off the vampire's head. Another was to burn a suspected vampire's body in its grave. But perhaps the best-known method was to drive a wooden stake through the creature's heart.

These methods were also believed to do more than just kill vampires. It was often thought that killing them this way helped **redeem** the monsters' souls so they could have a restful death. But it was never easy to destroy vampires. Folklore states that they were almost always alert and ready to fight intruders in their lairs.

redeem—to free from the consequences of sinful behavior

FACT: In 1486 the Christian church published a book called *Malleus Maleficarium*. It described how vampires were connected to the devil. The book also provided advice for how to deal with the demonic creatures. By the 1600s the *Malleus Maleficarium* became a guidebook to vampire hunters across Europe.

Medieval tales about vampire hunters were probably the inspiration for the most famous vampire hunter of all time. Professor Abraham Van Helsing was the main hunter in Bram Stoker's famous novel *Dracula*. Van Helsing set the standard for how vampire hunters are portrayed in many modern movies, TV shows, and books.

Van Helsing was very intelligent and used several vampire hunting tools. Besides garlic, holy water, and a crucifix, he also carried a mirror to learn a vampire's true nature. In the story, vampires had no soul, so they had no reflection in the mirror. Van Helsing's toolkit also included a wooden stake and hammer.

A vampire hunter's kit included several weapons, such as crucifixes, holy water, a mirror, and wooden stakes.

CHAPTER 4
Vampires Today

People have long been fascinated with tales of gruesome vampires. But these dynamic monsters have changed over time. While they were once evil and bloodthirsty monsters, vampires in today's stories are often seen as kindhearted heroes.

EARLY WRITINGS

In 1819 British physician John Polidori wrote one of the first popular vampire books. Simply titled *The Vampyre*, it featured Lord Ruthven, a dashing nobleman who hungered for blood. Ruthven used his natural charm to gain people's trust. But when people let him into their homes, he would attack them violently.

Another popular early novel was *Varney the Vampire: or, The Feast of Blood*. James Malcolm Rymer wrote it in 1847. Varney was the first vampire with several classic vampire traits. He is described as being tall, ugly, and very pale. He also has long fangs and fingernails. He often attacks women and even turns some of them into vampires. The novel became very popular in the mid-1800s. Varney would later have a strong influence on the most popular vampire story of all time.

FACT: *Varney the Vampire* was first published in England as a series of cheap pamphlets known as "penny dreadfuls." There were 220 issues in the original series. When it was published as one book, it was nearly 900 pages long.

DRACULA

Bram Stoker's 1897 book *Dracula* is the most famous vampire story ever written. The character of Count Dracula has strongly influenced vampires in books, films, and TV shows for more than 100 years. Dracula's powers and abilities captured people's imaginations. Because he has no soul, he doesn't have a shadow and has no reflection in mirrors. He has the power to control nature and the ability to scale castle walls. He can even walk around in full daylight and not be harmed. However, Dracula has to sleep in his native Transylvanian soil to maintain his powers.

Bram Stoker was inspired by the ruined abbey and graveyard in Whitby, England. Part of his novel Dracula *is set in this small English town.*

Stoker's novel brought more attention to vampires than any previous story. Dracula soon became the model upon which most authors based their vampires. Many vampires in modern tales have the same powers and abilities as Count Dracula.

FACT: In Stoker's novel, Count Dracula appears quite ugly. He has hairy palms, bad breath, and wears odd clothing. But his appearance later changed in films and stage plays. In the 1931 film *Dracula*, he is seen as a classy nobleman and even wears a tuxedo and cape.

EVOLUTION OF THE VAMPIRE

Modern vampires have even become heroes in many recent books, films, and TV shows. They are concerned about the safety of their human friends and are able to hold back their evil natures. They want to "do the right thing" in spite of being vampires. For example, they often choose to drink animal blood instead of attacking humans.

Modern vampires are also often more attractive than the gruesome monsters of the past. They don't have claws or fangs. They wear normal clothes and don't look like **corpses**. Modern vampires also don't seem to age. They instead seem to stay young and good-looking forever.

corpse—a dead body

The TV show Angel *featured a vampire who had regained his soul. He fought to protect innocent people from bloodthirsty vampires and other evil creatures.*

Although a few modern vampires are heroic, many others are still evil. They are dark, moody, and soulless creatures. These evil vampires are often cunning and always dangerous. They'll stop at nothing to get the blood and power they want. In most of these stories, heroic vampires are often the only ones able to stop evil vampires' wicked plans.

VAMPIRES THROUGH THE AGES

From ancient tales to modern pop culture, vampires have played an important role in our stories. While vampires have always had a dark side, they have appeared differently over time. They're often terrifying creatures that attack people to satisfy their hunger for blood. But sometimes they're seen as good-looking heroes who fight to protect humans.

Unlike people in ancient or medieval times, we no longer believe that vampires are real creatures. But people today still enjoy being scared by these bloodsucking monsters. New books about vampires are often best sellers. And movie theatres are often packed with vampire fans who want to see the latest hit film. It seems that no matter how terrifying they are, people can't get enough of their favorite bloodsucking monsters.

FACT: In the 1960s the TV show *The Munsters* showed vampires living like normal people. Count Vladimir Dracula, also known as Grandpa Munster, was a scientist. But he was also a 378-year-old vampire with a pet Transylvanian bat named Igor. His daughter Lily was also a vampire. She spent her days as a homemaker and mother.

VAMPIRES IN POPULAR CULTURE

TITLE	GOOD/EVIL	MEDIA	YEAR
Nosferatu	evil	film	1922
Dracula	evil	film	1931
The Addams Family	good	TV	1964–1966
The Munsters	good	TV	1964–1966
Dark Shadows	both	TV	1966–1971
The Monster Squad	evil	film	1987
Buffy the Vampire Slayer	both	TV	1997–2003
Castlevania	evil	video game	1999
Angel	both	TV	1999–2004
Twilight	both	novels/films	2005–2012
Hotel Transylvania	good	film	2012

In Buffy the Vampire Slayer, *Spike first appears as an evil vampire. But over time he becomes a good and heroic character.*

Glossary

baptize (BAP-tize)—to pour water on someone as part of a Christian religious practice

corpse (KORPS)—a dead body

crucifix (KROO-suh-fix)—a symbol of the beliefs of Christians

decompose (dee-kuhm-POHZ)—to rot or decay

folklore (FOLK-lor)—tales, sayings, and customs among a group of people

hypnotize (HIP-nuh-tize)—to put a person into a sleeplike state

impale (im-PALE)—to thrust a sharpened stake through a person's body

medieval (mee-DEE-vuhl)—having to do with the period of European history between AD 500 and 1450

mutilate (MYOO-tuh-late)—to seriously injure or damage someone or something

plague (PLAYG)—a disease that spreads quickly and kills most people who catch it

redeem (ri-DEEM)—to free from the consequences of sinful behavior

soul (SOLE)—the spiritual part of a person

trance (TRANSS)—a conscious state in which a person is not really aware of what is happening

undead (UN-ded)—no longer alive but still able to move and take action

Read More

Bailey, Diane. *Vampires in Mythology*. Vampires. New York: Rosen Central, 2012.

De'Ath, Otto. *The Vampire Hunter's Guide*. Monster Tracker. Mankato, Minn.: Sea-to-Sea Publications, 2012.

Felix, Rebecca. *Vampires.* Creatures Of Legend. Minneapolis: ABDO Publishing Company, 2014.

Owen, Ruth. *Vampires and Other Bloodsuckers*. Not Near Normal: The Paranormal. New York: Bearport Pub. Company, 2013.

Internet Sites

FactHound offers a safe, fun way to find Internet sites related to this book. All of the sites on FactHound have been researched by our staff.

Here's all you do:

Visit *www.facthound.com*

Type in this code: 9781491442500

Check out projects, games and lots more at
www.capstonekids.com

Index